RIDDLE ME THIS ONE

A TREASURY OF NEWFOUNDLAND TRIVIA

D1617593

JOHN W. DOYLE

BOULDER
PUBLICATIONS

Library and Archives Canada Cataloguing in Publication

Doyle, John (John William) author
    Riddle me this one: a treasury of Newfoundland trivia / John W. Doyle.

ISBN 978-1-927099-75-9 (paperback)

    1. Newfoundland and Labrador--Miscellanea. I. Title.

FC2161.6.D69 2016   971.8002   C2016-905587-6

Published by Boulder Publications
Portugal Cove-St. Philip's, Newfoundland and Labrador
www.boulderpublications.ca

© 2016 John W. Doyle

Design and layout: John Andrews
Editor: Stephanie Porter
Copy editor: Iona Bulgin

Printed in Canada

 We acknowledge the financial support of the Government of
Newfoundland Newfoundland and Labrador through the Department of Tourism,
Labrador Culture and Recreation.

We acknowledge the financial support for our publishing program by the Government of Canada and the Department of Canadian Heritage through the Canada
Book Fund.

Acknowledgements

Thanks to everyone who helped
with the research for this book:

Melvin Baker
Roger Bill
Norm Catto
Eric Colbourne
Barbara Doran
Marjorie M. Doyle
Philip Hiscock
Sandra LeFort
Mary Lewis
David Liverman
Patrick O'Flaherty
Carmel Parsons
Gerry Porter
Joan Ritcey
Paul Rowe
Paul Sparkes
Claire Wilkshire

Any errors are the author's.

Dedication

To my parents,
Mary (Foley) Doyle and
Gerald S. Doyle,
who cared for Newfoundland

Introduction

A friend said to me recently, "Newfoundland is not all that important in the grand scheme of things. But it sure is interesting." While I might disagree with the first point, I heartily concur with the second. For an island with a population of half a million, and a recorded history that only goes back half a millennium, Newfoundland has more than its fair share of interesting stories.

Where to begin? We have our own dictionary, running to 625 pages. We have an outsized presence in Canada's cultural landscape. Newfoundland has been a colony, a nation, and now a province—and through it all Newfoundlanders and Labradorians have maintained a reputation as talkers, entertainers, adventurers, and achievers.

This book is designed to both test and enrich your knowledge of Newfoundland and its ways. There are no trick questions, but the wording can be quite precise. Some questions require a general knowledge of Newfoundland history, culture, and traditions, but many can be answered using reason and common sense.

This book is about Newfoundland. Labrador has its own epic story, and I will leave the telling to writers whose roots are in the Big Land.

Newfoundland's history can be tangly, as they say. I have consulted wise people and tried to present a balanced view of controversial matters. But you know how it is.

A note to visitors: This book is for you, too. Some of the questions may be puzzling, but I trust you'll enjoy the answers.

Whatever your ties to the island, I hope this collection of Newfoundlandia brings you as much pleasure as I have had in compiling it.

MUSIC

Q

In a popular Newfoundland
folk song, what would
"kill a man twice after eating a slice"?

Q

Which Newfoundland singer-songwriter
was described by the *National Post* as
"a bit like Leonard Cohen being channeled
in a dusty saloon by Patsy Cline"?

A

The Trinity Cake.

A

Amelia Curran.

Six Shooter Records

Q

The 2005 Great Big Sea album
The Hard and the Easy takes its name from
a popular Newfoundland folk song.
What is the song?

Q

What band was the main act at the
1993 concert where Great Big Sea
played its first official gig?

"Tickle Cove Pond," by Mark Walker.

In cutting and hauling, in frost and in snow
We're up against troubles that few people know.
And only by patience, with courage and grit
And eating plain food can we keep ourselves fit.
The hard and the easy we take as it comes
And when ponds freeze over we shorten our runs.

Tickle Cove Pond

A

Great Big Sea opened for
The Irish Descendants at a
Memorial University concert.

Q

Which singer-songwriter released the first
album composed of totally original
content by a Newfoundland artist?
(Hint: the album came out in 1972.)

A

Ron Hynes: *Discovery*.

Q

In a popular Newfoundland
folk song, who was "wise Kitty"
and what was her advice?

A

"Wise Kitty" was the horse in
"Tickle Cove Pond" who, by her
actions, urged her owner not to take
a shortcut across spring ice.

One evening in April, bound home with a load,
The mare showed some halting against the ice road,
And knew more than I did as matters turned out
And lucky for me had I joined in her doubt.
She turned round her head, and with tears in her eyes,
As if she were saying: "You're risking our lives."

Q

Fill in the missing words
in this Joan Morrissey song:

I'll tell you a tale about Newfoundland dear
We haven't got money or riches to spare
But we can be thankful for one small affair
Thank God we're _____.

A

"Surrounded by water."
The song was adapted by Tom Cahill
from an Irish freedom song,
"The Sea Round Us."

Q

Which of these is *not* the title of a
contemporary Newfoundland song?

a. "Working in the Cold Storage"
b. "In Pursuit of the Wild Bologna"
c. "Aunt Martha's Sheep"
d. "The Crackie Ate the Mountie"
e. "The Liquor Continues to Flow"

A

d. "The Crackie Ate the Mountie" is the made-up title. The others are real:

"Working in the Cold Storage," written and recorded by Pierce Cull

"In Pursuit of the Wild Bologna" by Jamie Snider, recorded by Red Island

"Aunt Martha's Sheep" by Ellis Coles, recorded by Dick Nolan

"The Liquor Continues to Flow," by Gary Burton, and recorded by Susan Lawrence, is actually a pro-temperance song:

Oh the liquor has washed away our love dear,
Like a flood, it's wrecked our happy home.
And I thought that I could change your ways dear,
But the liquor, it continues to flow.

Q

Match the lyrics to the songwriter:

a. I'd give my food and drink to see my home again, to see my mother's hand against her apron edge

Ron Hynes & Joel Thomas Hynes

b. With everything gone, you could see everything

Lizband & Barry Newhook

c. I don't come with no disclaimer, I'm like everybody else

Colleen Power

d. She had a diamond as big as your eye … talk of war around the world could almost make her cry

Tim Baker

e. I wanted to use my imagination, but you said you didn't think I should

Amelia Curran

A

a. Tim Baker, "Carry Me Home"

b. Ron Hynes & Joel Thomas Hynes, "Dark River"

c. Amelia Curran, "The Mistress"

d. Lizband & Barry Newhook, "Complacency Song"

e. Colleen Power, "Happy Girlfriend"

Q

What is unusual about the
"Ode to Newfoundland"
compared to other national anthems?

Q

Supply the missing word(s) in these lyrics
from Roy Payne's 1969 hit song:

Surrounded by a mighty sea,
there's an island dear to me,
Described by some a place of rock and sand;
But so many a man has found when the world has
turned him down,
There's no _____
on the doors of Newfoundland.

A

It's largely about the weather.
Most other anthems extol the nation's
glorious past or military might.

A

"Price tags."

It was a different era. "No Price Tags on the
Doors of Newfoundland" was the title song
on Roy Payne's first album, which also
included "I Wouldn't Take a Million
Dollars for a Single Maple Leaf."

Payne went on to compose the musical
score for Dan Aykroyd's first film,
Love at First Sight (1977).

Q

According to family tradition,
John V. Devine composed
"The Badger Drive" in 1912 to

a. win the heart of a King's Cove woman
b. win back a job from which he had
   been fired
c. win a wager
d. win a place in the Newfoundland Folk
   Music Hall of Fame

A

b. Devine, a King's Cove man, was fired from his job in the woods camps with the Anglo-Newfoundland Development Company (for reasons lost to history). With a St. Patrick's Day concert coming up in Grand Falls, Devine composed a song praising both the skill of the log drivers and the qualities of the managers.

Another tradition says Devine was challenged by a logger who complained that fishermen had all the good Newfoundland songs. In any event, he got his job back. The song was said to be a favourite of Newfoundland folk song collector Gerald S. Doyle, Devine's nephew.

Q

What do these Newfoundlanders
have in common?

Wilf Doyle
Harry Hibbs
Ray Johnson
Daniel Payne
Art Stoyles
Minnie White

A

They are all known as outstanding
accordion players.

SingSong Inc.

ARTS & ENTERTAINMENT

Q

True or False:
Allan Hawco made his screen debut in
the underground film *Every Inch a Sailor*
while he was attending National
Theatre School in Montreal.

CBC

A

False.
Hawco's first film appearance
was in Mary Lewis's 1998 film
When Ponds Freeze Over.

Mary Lewis

Q

Which of these is not the title of a book
published in this province?

a. *Doctor, When You're Sick You're Not Well*
b. *Sposin' I Dies in D'Dory*
c. *The Fish Splitter's Daughter*
d. *Hard as Ice*
e. *Come Near at Your Peril*

A

c. *The Fish Splitter's Daughter* is bogus (but would probably do well on the book club circuit). The others are real:

Doctor, When You're Sick You're Not Well
(1998) by Gary Saunders

Sposin' I Dies in D'Dory
(1977) by Victor Butler

Hard as Ice
(2014) by Victoria Barbour,
book 2 in the Heart's Ease series

Come Near at Your Peril
(1994) by Patrick O'Flaherty

Why was Don Wright's sculpture
"The Red Trench" removed from
Confederation Building, and where
does it hang now?

A

Some people found the sculpture "offensive."
It now hangs in the atrium of the
Arts and Administration Building at
Memorial University of Newfoundland.

Q

What makes radio stations VOAR
and VOWR unique in Canada?

Q

What makes radio stations
VOAR, VOWR, and VOCM
unique in Canada?

A

They are the only radio stations in Canada
owned by a religious denomination.
The CRTC does not permit religious
denominations to own radio or television
stations, but VOAR and VOWR existed
before Newfoundland joined Canada, and
were grandfathered in. VOAR stands for
Voice of Adventist Radio; VOWR, Voice
of Wesleyan Radio.

A

They are the only Canadian radio stations
whose call signs begin with the letter V
(all the rest begin with the letter C).
These stations were on the air before
Confederation, when all Newfoundland
stations had V call signs.

Q

How many of the 161 inductees to
Canada's Walk of Fame in Toronto
are Newfoundlanders?

a. 1
b. 2
c. 3
d. 4

Canada's Walk of Fame by Simcoe St. *Wikimedia Commons/CC-SA-3.0*

A

a. The one and only Gordon Pinsent.

Q

True or false:
The hit Newfoundland feature film
The Grand Seduction was adapted
from the Newfoundland novel
of the same name.

Brendan Gleeson and Gordon Pinsent in *The Grand Seduction*.
Morag Loves Company

A

False. It was adapted from a Quebec film of the same name, *La Grande Séduction*.

Mary Walsh, Gordon Pinsent, and Brendan Gleeson. *Morag Loves Company*

Q

The frescoes that decorate the ceilings of Government House in St. John's were painted by:

a. British painter J.M.W. Turner on a visit to Newfoundland in 1843

b. A prisoner serving time at H.M. Penitentiary in 1880

c. Lady Grace Champneys, wife of the governor of Newfoundland (1909–13)

d. Noted Newfoundland artist Christopher Pratt in 1967

Newfoundland and Labrador Heritage Web Site (heritage.nf.ca)

A

b. They were painted in 1880 by the Polish fresco painter Alexander Pindikowski, who had come to Newfoundland to teach art in Heart's Content but was arrested for attempting to cash forged cheques. He was convicted of forgery and sentenced to 15 months in the penitentiary. His sentence was shortened by one month in return for painting the frescoes.

Newfoundland and Labrador Heritage Web Site (heritage.nf.ca)

Q

What do these cultural workers
have in common?

Marthe Bernard, Petrina Bromley,
Jordan Canning, Steve Cochrane,
Amelia Curran, Karyn Dwyer,
Didi Gillard Rowlings, Johnny Harris,
Allan Hawco, Christopher House,
Cathy Jones, Bob Joy, Jillian Keiley,
Susan Kent, Adriana Maggs,
Rick Mercer, Caroline Niklas-Gordon,
Mark O'Brien, Krystin Pellerin,
Nik Sexton, Sebastian Spence, Kate Story,
Nicole Underhay, Sherry White.

A

They all left Newfoundland for work.
(Based on a list of 236 names compiled by
Mary MacDonald for *The Overcast*.)

Q

Which of the following is not the name of
a TV series produced in Newfoundland?

    a. *Above and Beyond*
    b. *Dooley Gardens*
    c. *Hatching, Matching*
       and Dispatching
    d. *Pearson's Peak*
    e. *Random Passage*

A

d. *Pearson's Peak* is not a TV series
(but the name will come up again later).

Above and Beyond (2006) was a miniseries
about Gander's role in World War II

Dooley Gardens (1999) was a comedy set
in a St. John's rink

Hatching, Matching and Dispatching
(2005) was about a family-run wedding,
ambulance, and funeral services company
in a Newfoundland town

Random Passage (2002) was a miniseries
based on two novels by Bernice Morgan

Q

Where and when did the worst film crew
accident in North America occur?

Q

Who was Newfoundland's
first published novelist?

    a. Percy Janes
    b. Margaret Duley
    c. Al Pittman
    d. David French
    e. Anastasia English

A

Off the coast of Newfoundland in 1931
during the production of *The Viking*,
a feature film about the seal hunt. A
dynamite explosion on location killed
28 crew members, including the
director, Varick Frissell.
The film was released anyway.

A

Anastasia English. Her debut novel
Only a Fisherman's Daughter was
published in 1899. English was born
in St. John's and educated by the
Presentation Sisters. Two of her novels
have recently been republished by
Boulder Publications (*Only a Fisherman's
Daughter* in 2009 and *The Curse
of Flowervilla* in 2013).

Q

True or False: The movie *Maudie*,
starring Sally Hawkins and Ethan Hawke,
tells the story of Newfoundland's
greatest folk artist.

Duncan de Young/Mongrel

Q

In the fictional world of the 1990s
radio show *The Great Eastern*, why did
the Broadcasting Corporation of
Newfoundland's radio transmitter
produce a particularly warm sound?

A

False.
Although *Maudie* was shot in
Newfoundland from a script by
Newfoundlander Sherry White,
Maud Lewis was a Nova Scotia artist.

A

The BCN transmitter was coal-powered.

Q

Match the text to the author:

a. No one had ever needed a megaphone to speak the truth.

Michael Crummey

b. She is a woman who has played many parts in her life but is at last content to be no one other than herself.

Edward Riche

c. He ended his time on the shore in a makeshift asylum cell, shut away with the profligate stink of fish that clung to him all his days.

Wayne Johnston

Lisa Moore

d. My father grew up in a house that was blessed with water from an iceberg.

Joan Clark

e. They are silver arrows they are eels they are licorice they are Lycra they are muscle they are will and will not and want to be and winning.

Margaret Duley

f. She felt her veins rippling with life, and the wingspread of her spirit craving infinite future.

A

a. Edward Riche, *Rare Birds*
b. Joan Clark, *An Audience of Chairs*
c. Michael Crummey, *Galore*
d. Wayne Johnston, *Baltimore's Mansion*
e. Lisa Moore, *Flannery*
f. Margaret Duley, *Cold Pastoral*

Q

True or False:
Researchers at Cape Breton University
have discovered "troubling similarities"
between *Anne of Green Gables* and a
1907 children's book by a retired
Birchy Bay librarian.

Q
Who is this iconic member of the
Newfoundland arts community,
seen here in a 1982 NIFCO film?

A

False.

A

Andy Jones—actor, writer, director, and a founding member of CODCO. He played the pope in *Extraordinary Visitor 1982*, an early production from Newfoundland Independent Filmmakers Cooperative (NIFCO), which was founded in 1975 and continues to be a pillar of the provincial film and television industry.

Q

Name the Qalipu photographer who produced a series of portraits of Newfoundland and Irish people who share the same family names.

A

Sheilagh O'Leary. In 2004, O'Leary travelled the Irish Loop photographing people with Irish family names. Then she visited the Irish counties of Waterford, Wexford, and Kilkenny to shoot portraits of people with the same names. The exhibition *Twinning Lines* has been shown in St. John's and Waterford. O'Leary is a member of the Qalipu First Nation through her mother's Mi'kmaq heritage.

Ed Coady of Ireland and Ed Coady of Newfoundland and Labrador. *Sheilagh O'Leary, www.sheilagholeary.com*

HISTORY &
POLITICS

Q

Which statement is associated
with which premier?

a. "One day the sun will shine
   and have-not will be no more."
b. "There's no crisis."
c. "And that's backupable."
d. "We got it!"
e. "Burn your boats!"

A

a. Brian Peckford was partly right:
   have-not briefly was not.

b. Kathy Dunderdale assured
   Newfoundlanders during #DarkNL that
   everything was under control.

c. Tom Rideout coined the word
   "backupable" during a pre-election
   television debate. (His campaign slogan
   was "Ride In! Right On! Rideout!")

d. Danny Williams got it—"it" being a
   $2.6 billion deal with Ottawa. Williams
   also revived the phrase to announce the
   return of AHL hockey to St. John's.

e. Although Joey Smallwood always denied
   telling fishermen to burn their boats,
   the phrase is strongly associated with
   him. He did promise Newfoundlanders
   a brighter future through industrialization.

Q

How many of the first 10 premiers
of the province of Newfoundland
and Labrador were Townies
(i.e., born in St. John's)?

A

One—Danny Williams.

Joey Smallwood: Mint Brook
Frank Moores: Carbonear
Brian Peckford: Whitbourne
Tom Rideout: Fleur de Lys
Clyde Wells: Buchans Junction
Brian Tobin: Stephenville
Beaton Tulk: Ladle Cove
Roger Grimes: Grand Falls-Windsor
Kathy Dunderdale: Burin

Q

Who was premier when the name of
the province was officially changed to
"Newfoundland and Labrador"?

Q

Who was premier of Newfoundland
when the word "and" was dropped from
the province's official logo?

A

Roger Grimes (December 6, 2001).
The process began under Brian Tobin.

A.

Danny Williams (2006).

Q.

True or False:
The provincial government once published an official book of cucumber recipes to offset the low consumption of the vegetable in Newfoundland and Labrador.

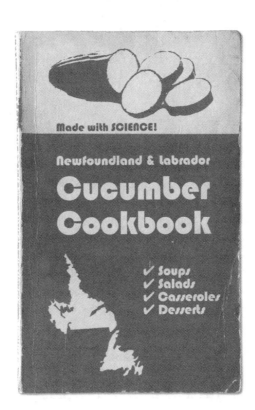

A

True, although the real cover is not as flashy. The 1988 book was compiled by Beverley Sprung and has an aerial shot of the eponymous greenhouses on the cover. The recipes include Cucumber Amandine and Lemon Cucumber Jelly Salad ("A nice light salad you will enjoy serving with many dishes—and so easy!").

The real cover of *Cucumber Recipes*.

Q

True or False:
Premier J.R. Smallwood's ideas about
outport resettlement were heavily
influenced by a meeting with Leon Trotsky
at the Cochrane Hotel in St. John's in
1917. The cub reporter interviewed the
revolutionary for the St. John's *Plaindealer*.

A

Probably false.
The photo is fake (courtesy John Andrews), but Trotsky may have stayed in St. John's, and young Smallwood was trying to get into the newspaper game at the time.

The plaque on Cochrane House, St. John's.

Q

When the last British governor of
Newfoundland left the country in 1949,
the *Evening Telegram* published a short
poem in praise of Sir Gordon Macdonald.
Shortly after the paper hit the streets,
the poem was the talk of the town.
Why did it spark such a strong reaction?

"LABORER".

FAREWELL

Dear Mr. Editor,—Would you publish attached farewell to His Excellency Sir Gordon Macdonald, K.C.M.G.

A Farewell!

The prayers of countless thousands
    sent
Heavenwards to speed thy safe re-
    turn,
Ennobled as thou art with duty
    well performed,
Bringing peace, security and joy
Among the peoples of this New
    Found Land.
So saddened and depressed until
    your presence
Taught us discern and help decide
    what's best for
All on whom fortune had not
    smiled.
Remember if you will the kindness
    and the love
Devotion and the rest that we the
    people have for Thee—Fare-
    well!
         —E. A.

PROTEST OIL COATED STREET

A

The poem was an acrostic: the first letters
in each line spell THE BASTARD.
Governor Macdonald was not universally
liked. Historians are divided on whether
the newspaper got punked, or the editors
were in cahoots with the author.

Q

What is going on in this 2006 federal government photograph?

Atlantic Canada Opportunities Agency (ACOA) photo

A

The official story: The Honourable Peter
MacKay, Minister of Foreign Affairs and
Minister of the Atlantic Canada Opportunities
Agency, joined colleague Fabian Manning,
MP Avalon, for the official re-opening of
the tourism attraction Father Duffy's Well.
The real story: two federal politicians attempt
to look like ordinary fun guys by hijacking their
own photo op to make crude use of a revered
spiritual site. Father Duffy's Well had been known
for its healing powers since 1835, when a thirsty priest
struck a rock and water gushed forth. However, an
old text warns that the well's miraculous powers
would not survive inappropriate use:

Cursed be the man that dare profane
This loved and sacred shrine,
And make excuse "material use"
So callous is our time.
Commercial use may dollars bring
But never can excel
The sentimental heritage
Of Father Duffy's well.

(No miracles have been reported at Father
Duffy's Well since the photograph was taken.)

Q

What Newfoundland community is the
only union-built town in Canada, and one
of the few in North America?

Photo David Burt, DBA Consulting Engineers Ltd.

A

Port Union, Trinity Bay.
The town was founded in 1916 by William
F. Coaker as the headquarters of the Fishermen's Protective Union. It was a decidedly
modern community with a hydroelectric
generating station, a fish plant with electric
salt-fish dryers, and a printing press for
the weekly *Fishermen's Advocate*. Some
of the original buildings have been restored
and newspaper buffs will be delighted
to find an intact Linotype typesetting
machine on display.

Photo on previous page shows the
recontructed and restored historic Port
Union fish plant and retail store.

Q

When did Newfoundland switch
from driving on the left side of the road
to driving on the right?

a. September 12, 1901
b. January 1, 1934
c. June 1, 1941
d. January 2, 1947
e. April 1, 1949

Q

True or False:
In 1948 the Turks and Caicos Islands
sent a delegation to London to explore the
possibility of union with Newfoundland.
The overture was seen as an attempt to
join Canada by the back door, and was
vetoed by the British government.

A

d. The switch was made on January 2, rather than the more obvious January 1, because authorities were concerned about New Year's Eve revellers who might not be in any fit state to deal with the confusion.

Wisely, the authorities also rejected suggestions that the changeover be phased in over a week. The reason the switch happened in 1947 is lost in the mists of time.

A

False.
There has been sporadic talk of the Islands joining Canada for a century, but only Nova Scotia has ever reached out to suggest union.

Q

In what year did Newfoundland adopt
the dollar as its currency?

a. 1863
b. 1918
c. 1929
d. 1949

Q

Who was the first woman elected to the
Newfoundland House of Assembly?

A

a. 1863
Prior to this Newfoundland used
pound notes and a variety of coins.

A

Helena Squires, elected in 1930
in the district of Lewisporte.

Q

True or False:
According to his authorized biographer, former premier Frank Moores acquired his nickname "The Rowdy Man" at an after party organized by John Lennon following a benefit concert in aid of a New York State mental facility in 1975.

A

False.
The photo is fake (courtesy Gerry Porter),
and while Moores and Lennon could
conceivably have met in 1975, his
nickname was already well established.

Q

How long was Newfoundland a country before becoming a province of Canada?

a. From 1832 to 1934
b. From 1855 to 1934
c. From 1907 to 1949
d. Never

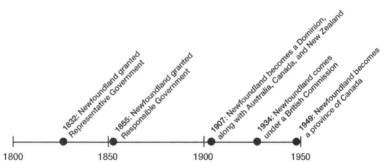

A

Take your pick.
You can find a historian to defend
any of those statements, including
"never." Much depends upon how you
define "country."

Note to visitors: this subject is best avoid-
ed in the company of Newfoundlanders,
especially if drink has been taken.

Q

True or False:
During the Cold War the US Navy
operated a secret submarine listening
post near St. Anthony.

A

False, but not far off: The American listening post was at Naval Station Argentia. Cables snaked out under the sea for 20 kilometres to track Soviet submarines. The Soviets in turn sent a spy to find out more about the top-secret technology, but he was caught in a sting operation conducted over fish and chips.

Accused spy pleads guilty

U.S. sting operation began on Soviet "research" ship

By BERNIE BENNETT
of The Evening Telegram

The Newfoundland Supreme Court heard Monday how a female officer from the U.S. Naval Facility at Argentia set up an elaborate sting operation to catch a Soviet "research" ship in St. John's harbor — and trapped Stephen Joseph Ratkai.

The 25-year-old Antigonish, N.S. native entering a surprise plea of guilty plea on two charges of spying for the Russians.

Then he sat back, looking relaxed, in the prisoner's docket to listen to a six-hour recitation by an RCMP officer of the details of an undercover operation leading to Mr. Ratkai's arrest last June 11 at Hotel Newfoundland.

He had pleaded not guilty to three charges of espionage and one charge of attempted espionage, each carrying a maximum of 14 years imprison.

The plea was changed to guilty after the Crown reduced the charges to one count of espionage and one of attempted espionage.

Earlier, Mr. Ratkai re-elected trial by judge without a jury, a change from his original choice of judge and jury. With that, Mr. Justice Vivian Aylward thanked the 125 people who showed up after being summoned for jury duty and allowed them to leave.

As each of the two charges were read Mr. Ratkai responded in a loud, firm voice with "Guilty."

He assured the court that the choice of pleading guilty was made of his own free will without any promises or threats of any kind.

With the unexpected twist to Newfoundland's first ever espionage trial, Crown prosecutor Gordon MacRah, assisted by law partner James Vavasour, said the statement of facts and pre-sentence report would take four or five days to complete — compared to the month — long trial that had been anticipated.

See RCMP, Page 2

Volume 110 — Number 260

The E

Tuesday, February 7, 1989

Public on fisl

By JOE WALSH
of The Evening Telegram

There has been a call by a spokesman for inshore fishing interests for a public inquiry into the management of the northern cod fish stock.

And Cabot Martin, president of the Newfoundland Inshore Fisheries Association (NIFA), said Monday public participation should begin this Wednesday when the Atlantic Groundfish Advisory Committee (AGAC) meets at the Radisson Plaza Hotel in St. John's.

He sees pressure from the various interest groups has led to the decline of the valuable fish stock.

ENTERS COURT
Stephen Ratkai is led to the court house in St. John's Monday just before he pleaded guilty to charges of espionage and attempted espionage. The court will continue hearing sentencing evidence today.

The Evening Telegram, *February 7, 1989*

Q

Which of the following was not mentioned in the Terms of Union when Newfoundland became part of Canada in 1949?

a. The fisheries
b. The Gulf ferry
c. Unemployment Insurance
d. The status of indigenous people
e. Margarine

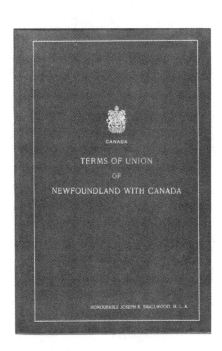

A

d. The agreement makes no mention of any indigenous people living in Newfoundland or Labrador. The omission would have troubling long-term implications.

Q

What did the Commission of Government establish at Markland in 1934?

Q

Where were the first oil wells in Newfoundland?

A

A farming community. The Commission saw agriculture as a way to create employment and lessen dependency on the dole. Families received assistance to develop farmland in previously uninhabited areas.

A

Parsons Pond. A Nova Scotian named John Silver started the rush in 1867 when he heard about oil slicks on local ponds. Oil was pumped and refined there on and off until 1926. (Some say Parsons Pond was named after a visiting parson who found the oil helpful with his rheumatism.)

Q

Which colour is closest to the flagpole
when the Pink, White, and Green is flown?

Q

True or False:
The Markland farm community included
an experimental non-denominational
"folk school," where the curriculum
included carpentry, farming, and fishing.

A

Green.

A

False.
Fishing was not part of the
curriculum. The school was intended
to foster a self-sustaining lifestyle and,
in Depression-era Newfoundland,
fishing was viewed as part of the
problem, not the solution.

Q

True or False:
The Newfoundland Tricolour
is the oldest flag in the world
to use the colour pink.

A

True.

The history of the Pink, White, and Green
is still the subject of scholarly debate. In
the absence of an agreed version of the
facts, here's one of the myths:

It was the winter of 1835. Harsh condi-
tions had stoked ill feeling between the
Protestant English and Catholic Irish.
Bishop Michael Anthony Fleming, out for
one of his legendary walks in the country, came upon two parties of woodsmen
feuding over their hauls of firewood. The
Catholics had marked their pile with
a green flag, the Protestants with pink.
Fleming called for the two flags to be
brought to him. Tearing a strip of silk
from his surplice, he bound the green and
pink together with the white flag of truce
and proclaimed, "Let this be your flag!"

Q

Which of these jurisdictions was the last to declare women's suffrage?

a. Canada
b. Newfoundland
c. United States of America
d. New Zealand

A

b. Newfoundland, in 1925.

Newfoundland and Labrador suffragists, ca. 1920. *Archives and Special Collections Division, Coll. 158 8.11, Memorial University of Newfoundland*

Q

True or False:
Newfoundland is the oldest European
name for a Canadian place in continuous
literary and cartographic use.

Q

Fill in the missing word(s)
in this political slogan:
We'll finish the drive in '65 thanks to

_____.

A

True.
The first reference is in a letter dated 1502.

A

Mr. Pearson.
Premier Smallwood used the slogan
to trumpet his deal with the federal
government to pay 90 per cent of the
cost of completing the Trans-Canada
Highway on the island.

Q

Which of these was once considered
part of Newfoundland?

a. Anticosti Island
b. Cape Breton Island
c. Magdalen Islands
d. Sable Island
e. Saint-Pierre and Miquelon

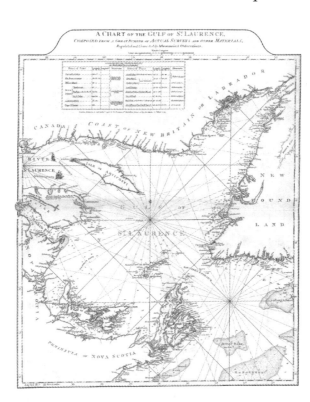

A

a. Anticosti Island was annexed
to Newfoundland twice in the
18th and 19th centuries.

Q

What did fisherman Gus Dalton
discover when he set out from St. Shott's
on the morning of August 11, 1986,
to tend his nets?

Q

It is December 21, 1933. Newfoundland's
ruling elite has gathered in the ballroom
of the Newfoundland Hotel for a lavish
banquet. Guests feast on grilled lamb and
poached salmon while Newfoundland's
last prime minister reads a telegram from
London confirming that Newfoundland's
independence has been suspended. Speak-
ers present Prime Minister Alderdice with a
clock and a pair of silver candlesticks.

Is this:
a. a historical account
b. a scene from a
    Wayne Johnston novel

A

Two lifeboats carrying Tamil refugees
who had been put overboard from a
freighter by human smugglers. Dalton
and his fellow fishermen rescued all
155 people.

A

a. The banquet was sponsored by the
ruling United Newfoundland Party to
honour Alderdice as he prepared to retire.

Q

What celebrated body of water did
Premier J.R. Smallwood use as a
comparison when boasting about the
size of the Smallwood Reservoir on
the Churchill River?

Joey Smallwood, 1959. *Duncan Cameron/Library and Archives
Canada/PA-113253*

A

The Sea of Galilee.
Smallwood said the reservoir
was six times bigger.

NEWFOUNDLAND
CONNECTIONS

Q

True or False:
During World War I, Newfoundland
shoe factories supplied sealskin boots
to the British army.

Q

True or False:
The Labrador Retriever has
no connection to Labrador.

A

False.
Newfoundland companies did tender on the supply of boots, but were not successful. Some people sent sealskin boots to family members who were soldiers because they were more waterproof than standard military issue.

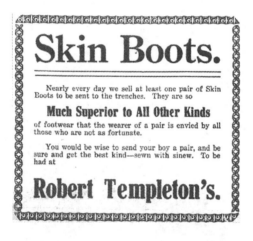

Skin Boots.

Nearly every day we sell at least one pair of Skin Boots to be sent to the trenches. They are so

Much Superior to All Other Kinds

of footwear that the wearer of a pair is envied by all those who are not as fortunate.

You would be wise to send your boy a pair, and be sure and get the best kind—sewn with sinew. To be had at

Robert Templeton's.

A

True.
The Labrador Retriever was bred in England in the 19th century from the St. John's water dog. This unregistered breed was also the foundation breed of most of the modern retrievers, such as the golden retriever.

Q

During World War I, volunteers in
Newfoundland gathered sphagnum
moss for shipment to England.
What was it used for?

Q

Which was the first mainstream
American TV soap opera to
mention Newfoundland?

A

The sphagnum was used for wound
dressings when supplies of cotton ran low.
The moss is naturally anti-bacterial,
a property that was long known to
indigenous North Americans.

A

The Young and the Restless in a July 2016
episode. The storyline concerned an oil
spill, and the dialogue included these lines:

Luca: He's been covering the Newman Oil
story since the beginning. He's on site now.
Summer: So he's in Newfoundland?
Luca: Yeah, he's been hitting up the local pubs,
drinking beers with the workers.

Q

What was this country music legend
doing in Newfoundland in 1961?

Q

True or False:
The Newfoundland dog
was not bred in Newfoundland.

A

Johnny Cash was hunting moose and posing with a Motorola Handie-Talkie two-way radio for magazine ads. (Years later Cash's son John Carter Cash would be arrested at Deer Lake airport for stripping down to his underwear, but that's another story.)

A

False.
The Newfoundland dog breed was created by Newfoundland fishermen who crossbred the St. John's water dog with mastiff breeds, most likely Portuguese mastiffs brought to the island by Portuguese fishermen.

A St. John's water dog at work.

Q

Which of the following famous dogs was a Newfoundland?

a. Nana, the dog in J.M. Barrie's *Peter and Wendy*
b. Napoleon the Wonder Dog, star of Van Hare's Magic Circus in 19th-century England
c. The fisherman's dog (name unknown) who saved Napoleon Bonaparte from drowning in 1815 off the island of Elba
d. Faithful, US president Ulysses S. Grant's dog
e. All of the above

A

e. All of the above.
(Disney's *Peter Pan* changed
Nana to a Saint Bernard.)

Q

What is the connection between the main entrance gates of McGill University and the Northern Peninsula town of Roddickton?

Q

True or False:
Divine Ryan is the stage name
of a Las Vegas exotic dancer
originally from Bonavista.

A

Both are named after Sir Thomas Roddick,
who was born in Harbour Grace and
became a celebrated Canadian surgeon
and dean of McGill's School of Medicine.

A

False.
But it's not too late.

Q

What Newfoundland folk song
was recorded by Bob Dylan?

Q

What famous Newfoundlander was
featured on Wheaties cereal boxes in 1940?

A

"The Bloomin' Bright Star of Belle Isle."
Dylan recorded the song as "Belle Isle" on
his 1970 album *Self Portrait*. He may have
first heard the song at the 1965 Newport
Jazz Festival, performed by Mrs. Annie
Walters of Rocky Harbour.

A

Captain Bob Bartlett, who had achieved in-
ternational fame for his Arctic voyages. Bartlett had mixed feelings about fame, although
it helped to fund his travel. He said, "It's all
right while you're exploring. You get used to
rotten meat, frozen fingers, lice, and dirt.
The hard times come when you get back."

"CHAMPS" OF THE U.S.A. SET NO. 9

CAPTAIN BOB BARTLETT
Famed explorer, hero of countless arctic ex-
peditions. Born in Brigus, Newfoundland.
Learned exploring under Peary. Captained
Coast Guard Ship Karluk in 1914, escaped
with 17 men to an island off Siberia after ice
crushed the Karluk! Crossed the ice to
Siberia for aid. Reached Nome, Alaska with
13 survivors a year later. Holds dozens of
medals, has authored three books.

Q

True or False:
In 2002 Pope John Paul II transformed the centuries-old Rosary by adding Five Luminous Mysteries to the traditional Joyful, Sorrowful, and Glorious Mysteries. The driving force behind the reform was Sister Mary Ellen Sellars, a Mercy nun originally from Springdale.

A

False.
The Luminous Mysteries did get added,
but there was no Springdale nun involved.
(Photo fakery by John Andrews.)

Q

Which of these products has never been
manufactured in Newfoundland?

a. artillery shells
b. guitars
c. chocolate bars
d. condoms
e. cigarettes
f. mustard pickles
g. cottage cheese

A

d. Rumours flew in the 1950s that Superior Rubber Products in Holyrood was producing condoms, prompting the Roman Catholic parish priest to warn his parishioners against taking a job at the plant, but it was a misunderstanding. The rubber boots which the factory produced during its brief life were said to be leaky, so it may be fortunate that the plant didn't make condoms.

Q

True or False: The 1960s famous
Whole Earth Catalog had its roots in
Newfoundland.

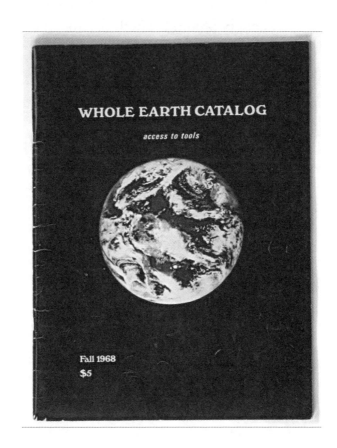

A

False.
But imagine if it had. Many
Newfoundlanders are gifted innovators
with tools and improvised solutions to
physical problems, which is what the
Catalog was all about.

Q

True or False:
The Gordon Pinsent Centre for the Arts
was a gift from the Czechoslovakian
government to the residents of central
Newfoundland in gratitude for their
rescue efforts when a Czech Airliner
crashed on takeoff from Gander
airport in 1967.

The Gordon Pinsent Centre for the Arts, Grand Falls-Windsor.
Pat Braden

A.

False.

The Centre (formerly the Grand Falls Arts & Culture Centre) does incorporate a large portion of the popular Czech pavilion at Expo 67, but it was purchased by the provincial government after the world's fair for 230,000 Czech Crowns. Other pieces of the pavilion were incorporated into the Joseph R. Smallwood Arts & Culture Centre in Gander.

Q.

True or False:
Cuban president Fidel Castro tried
tobogganing while on a stopover at
Gander airport.

Q

True or False:
In 1919 an English mathematician set up
an experiment on Bell Island to test Einstein's
Theory of Relativity during a solar eclipse.

A

True.
It was Christmas Eve 1976.

Ian Blackmore

A

False.
Sir Arthur Stanley Eddington travelled to
the island of Príncipe, off the west coast of
Africa, to conduct his experiment.

Q

True or False:
The zeppelin *Hindenburg* flew over
Newfoundland on May 5, 1937—
the day before it exploded in
Lakehurst, New Jersey.

A

True.
It was the *Hindenburg*'s
13th flight over the island.

Previous page photo:
Hindenburg over Brigus.
(The Rooms Provincial Archives Division,
Series VA 6; VA 7, Item VA 6-87)

Q

The Irish name for Newfoundland,
Talamh an Éisc, translates as:

      a. land of fish
      b. distant land
      c. miserable island
      d. new land

Q

What kind of research was Sir Frederick
Banting planning to discuss with scientists
in England when he was killed in a plane
crash near Musgrave Harbour in 1941?

      a. a cure for cancer
      b. an insulin nasal spray
      c. germ warfare
      d. genetic crop breeding
         techniques
      e. post-war reconstruction

A

a. Land of fish (or fishing grounds).

A

c. Germ warfare.
One of Banting's experiments involved
using sawdust emitted from low-flying
planes to spread weaponized microbes.

Q

True or False: *Melba toast* was named after Melba Toulinguet, the stage name of Newfoundland-born soprano Georgina Stirling.

Q

True or False: During World War II a schoolgirl found a German Enigma code machine hidden in a church attic in Trepassey.

A

False.
The woman known as the Nightingale
of the North performed as Marie
Toulinguet (after her hometown,
Twillingate). Melba toast was named after
Australian soprano Dame Nellie Melba.

A

False.
The story originates in a novel,
but circulates as a classic "urban legend"
involving a German agent impersonating
a village priest and local fishermen
capturing a U-boat.
(Photo courtesy Gerry Porter.)

NEWFOUNDLAND ENGLISH

Q

A Newfoundlander who drops the *h* in words like home and happy is more likely to be:

a. Catholic
b. Protestant

Q

True or False:
The use of the word *skeet* to describe "an ignorant, aggressive and unruly youth, of low education, often wearing sportswear, and associated with loitering, non-standard English language, drug and alcohol use, and petty crime" originated in Newfoundland.

A

b. Protestant. Deleting the voiceless glottal fricative is typical of English regional dialects. Newfoundlanders whose ancestors emigrated from England are likely to have been born into Protestant families or communities. Catholic Newfoundlanders are usually Irish descendants and tend to have other speech characteristics such as pronouncing thin like tin.

A

True. It may be related to the Prince Edward Island word *skite*, a young scoundrel. (Some language authorities consider skeet classist and advise against its use.)

Q

Which word has the longest entry in the
Dictionary of Newfoundland English?

Q

What do the terms *brickle*, *sish*, and
devil's blanket have in common?

A

"Fish." The second longest is "fishing."
They're used in many combined
forms such as "fish boil" (which is not
a meal) and "fishing room" (which is
not in a house).

A

They describe types of snow and ice.
Brickle is ice that is easily broken. *Sish*
is fine, granulated ice floating on the
surface of the sea. The *devil's blanket* is
a snowfall that keeps you from doing
your work. In her book *Brickle, Nish and
Knobbly: A Newfoundland Treasury of
Terms for Ice and Snow*, visual artist
Marlene Creates identifies 80 named
varieties of ice, snow, and winter weather
in Newfoundland English.

Q

According to the community's residents,
which is the correct way to pronounce
Francois?

a. like the French *François*
b. fran-sway (rhymes with slipway)
c. they don't really care

Q

What is a *damper dog*?

a. A tool for lifting the lids on an
   old-fashioned wood-burning
   kitchen stove
b. Another name for touton
c. A fisherman's canine companion
d. A sailor who tells stories in return
   for drink

A

b, but also c. Although most residents
say "fran-sway," they generally feel
it's much more important that people
stop talking about resettling the place.

A

b. Another name for touton, a simple
delicacy of fried bread dough.
The implication is that the dough
would be fried directly on top of the
stove rather than in a pan.

Q

What does *drung* mean?

a. extremely intoxicated
b. a variant past participle
   of the verb *dring*
c. a laneway
d. *wrong* or *incorrect* as in
   "you bought drung one"

Q

What's the traditional name for this type
of landscape feature?

A

c. A narrow lane or passage between
houses, fenced gardens, etc.
(*Dictionary of Newfoundland English*)

A

Tolt, "a prominent rounded hill rising
above the surrounding terrain"
(*Dictionary of Newfoundland English*). Tolt
is another of those old English words like
drung that survive only in Newfoundland.

Q

What are the more common
Newfoundland names for these berries?

a. mountain ash berry
b. lingonberry
c. saskatoon berry
d. cloudberry

A

a. dogberry
b. partridgeberry
c. chuckley pear
d. bakeapple

Why *bakeapple* for a small fruit that tastes nothing like apples? Several explanations have been offered:

- In warm sunny weather they smell like apple pie.
- It's a corruption of the French *baie qu'appelle*, which might be pidgin French for "What's the name of this berry?"
- It's a corruption of "bog apple."
- It comes from the Inuktitut word *aqpik*.

None of these explanations is entirely convincing.

Q

How many Newfoundland
accents are there?

a. one
b. two
c. at least a dozen
d. impossible to say

Q

What is the more common name
for the berries also known as *hurts*,
also spelled *whorts* (*Vaccinium* spp.)?

A

d. Newfoundland English largely
reflects the influences of England,
Ireland, and North America, but there
are local influences such as French on
the Port au Port Peninsula. For linguists
and folklorists there is no meaningful
way to count "accents."

A

Blueberries.
The older names come from
the English *hurtleberry*.

Q

What is the meaning of the
expression "an apostolic haul"?

a. a load of fish caught on a Sunday
b. the first catch of the year, when
blessed by a clergyman
c. an unusually large catch of fish
d. a net full of dogfish

Q

What is a *pissquick*?

a. a poorly maintained service
station washroom
b. a fisherman who can relieve
himself in all kinds of weather
c. a rubber boot cut off to form a
slip-on shoe

A

c. An unusually large catch of fish, from
the biblical reference to the apostle Simon:

Now when he had left speaking, he said unto
Simon, Launch out into the deep, and let down
your nets for a draught. And Simon answering
said unto him, Master, we have toiled all the
night, and have taken nothing: nevertheless at
thy word I will let down the net. And when they
had this done, they inclosed a great multitude of
fishes: and their net brake. (Luke 5:4–6 KJV)

This biblical quotation is also the source
of Memorial University's motto, *Provehito
in Altum*, variously translated as "Launch
forth into the deep" or "Close your eyes
and jump off the deep end" (the latter in
jest by Memorial's founding president,
John Lewis Paton).

A

c. The shoe would be easy to slip on
for a trip to the outhouse.

Q

True or False:
In parts of Western Newfoundland,
an "April Fool" is called an "April Fish,"
a literal translation of the French
expression *poisson d'avril*.

Q

What is the old Newfoundland term for
the medical condition *sleep paralysis with
hypnagogic hallucinations*?

A

False.

A

The Old Hag. Afflicted sleepers feel they are awake and able to hear but are unable to move. In Newfoundland folklore this is said to be the doing of a witch who sits on the sleeper's chest.

Q

A person who has
a head like a brewis bag ...

a. is forgetful
b. has an unusually large head
c. is soaked to the skin with
    salt water
d. has red hair

Q

What is the last entry in the
Dictionary of Newfoundland English?

A

a. The person is empty-headed or forgetful. A brewis bag is a cloth bag full of holes used to boil hard bread for the popular dish, fish and brewis (pronounced "brooze").

A

Zad, a variant pronunciation of the letter *Z*.

Q

Which comes first at a time,
a scoff or a scuff?

Q

What does it mean to say that someone
"smokes like a tilt"?

Q

True or False:
When Newfoundlanders say fish,
they generally mean cod.

A

Scuff before scoff, or you risk getting
a cramp. *Time* is a catch-all term for
various kinds of social occasions which
often include dancing (scuff) and
a late supper (scoff).

A

The person is a heavy smoker. A tilt is
a temporary shelter in the woods, and a
fire built inside would generate clouds
of smoke.

A

True.

CULTURE &
FOLKLORE

Q

True or False: There is no documented
case of anyone being buried with a picture
of Joey Smallwood in their coffin.

Q

In some Newfoundland versions of the
card game 120s, a player who bids 30-for-
60 on this hand is said to be "pulling a
Danny." Why?

A

True.

A

The play is named for former premier
Danny Williams. The hand is missing
the five of trumps, making the bid high-
ly risky. This recalls Williams's statement
that he had "a huge tolerance for risk."
He was talking about Muskrat Falls.

Q

Which of the following is said to be a way
to avoid being led astray by fairies?

a. Smoke two cigarettes at the same time
b. Keep a slice of bologna in your pocket
c. Turn your sweater inside-out
d. Recite The Lord's Prayer backwards

Q

What's wrong with this picture?

A

c. Turn your sweater inside-out.

A

Ill-mannered use of a bog bike
has laid waste to a lovely marsh.

Q

True or False:
The driving distance from St. John's to Port
aux Basques is longer than the reverse trip
on account of the generally northern
curvature of the Trans-Canada Highway
(in the same way that the outside lane of
a race track is longer than the inside).

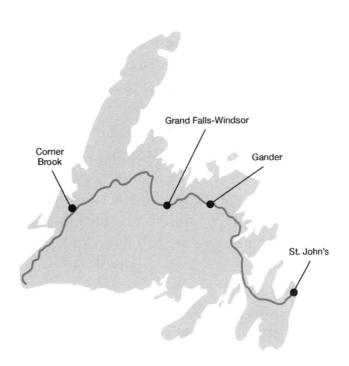

A

False.

According to Memorial University geography professor Dr. Norm Catto, although this theoretically could work out, it's not reliable because:

i. the relative difference in length between the outside and inside bends on a highway is much less than on a track, which has ~90° corners (difference decreases with shallower angles of curvature used on higher-speed routes);

ii. bends alternate in position, so statistically there could be as many right curves as left curves; it's the individual curves rather than the overall curvature of the highway that would make any potential difference (we see this in meandering rivers); and

iii. in the divided sections, the westbound and eastbound lanes might not be entirely parallel.

Q

What is May snow
thought to be good for?

Q

In 1993 a St. John's hair stylist assaulted a
client with a dryer because she thought he
was playing with himself under the cape.
What was he actually doing?

Q

How do mummers or jannies
disguise their voices?

A

Treating eye problems.

A

Cleaning his eyeglasses.

A

They talk on the in-breath.

Q

When the queen visited Newfoundland in 1997 for the Cabot Anniversary celebrations, Premier Brian Tobin was accused of committing a breach of royal protocol. What did the premier do?

Q

What was the most popular team sport in Newfoundland in the 1890s?

Q

True or False:
The delicacies known as cod tongues are not actually the tongues of codfish.

A

Tobin put his arm around Her Majesty's lower back as she was mounting the steps of Confederation Building. (One does not touch the sovereign, other than to exchange a limp handshake.)

A

Cricket. In the early 20th century it lost ground to soccer.

A

True.
Cod don't have tongues. Anatomically the tasty morsels are *basihyals*, a structure on the floor of the mouth that superficially resembles a tongue but doesn't have taste buds, isn't muscular, and has very little range of motion. It probably originally evolved to protect the ventral aorta, which lies very close to the mouth, from impacts with large, wriggly food.

Q

What was the paint manufacturer's
name for the shade of yellow traditionally
used on dories?

Newfoundland banking dory. *Adapted from canada-maps.org*

Q

Who created the
Republic of Newfoundland?

A

Dory Buff, produced in Newfoundland
for many years by Matchless Paints.

A

David "Snuffy" Jackson, a Texas-born
graphic artist who designed the first
Republic of Newfoundland T-shirt in 1982 as a
novelty product. Jackson lived in Newfoundland
during the 1980s, working as a musician, radio
host, and hairdresser. He never imagined
the confusion his design would create in the
popular history of Newfoundland.

14—THE DAILY NEWS, WEDNESDAY, JUNE 15, 1983

"Republic of Newfoundland"

Pro-separatist
T-shirts soon!

A new T-shirt will appear
on the market shortly that is
bound to please some people
and ruffle more than a few
feathers at the same time.

While the design is not
crude, rude or obscene, it will
possibly still be the cause of
some controversy.

Surrounding the old Pink,
White and Green
Newfoundland nationalist
tricolour, in large block
letters will be the words
"Republic of Newfoun-
dland."

While doubtless a hit with
nationalist, republican
separatists in Newfoundland,
the design is not expected to
please either the pro-
Canadian Newfoundlanders
or monarchists, whether they
are separatists or not.

The shirts were designed
by Dave Jackson of Harbour
City General Store, located
on the east side of the War

Q

True or False:
The first documented screech-in
ceremony took place in Brigus in 1813.

Q

True or False:
Under Roman Catholic law,
seals are officially fish.

A

False.
The first documented screech-in was held
at The Bella Vista in St. John's in 1976.

A

True.
Practically speaking, this means that
seal can be eaten on days when meat is
prohibited. Many Newfoundlanders
still refer to the "seal fishery."

Q

What does this pictogram mean?

a. Puffin crossing
b. No smoking
c. No puffin hunting
d. Puffin-free menu
e. Contains no puffin oil

A

b. No smoking (no puffin').

Q

Where would you find this unusually
literate sign?

A

At Burton's Pond on Memorial University's St. John's campus. The last sentence is a perfect example of wisely ending a sentence with a preposition.

Q

What is the common but possibly offensive term for this type of house entrance?

Q

True or False:
Chips, dressing, and gravy
is a Newfoundland specialty.

A

In-law door. Houses like this were built from approved plans which always included a front door, but many people were accustomed to using only the back door of their homes and saw no need to waste money on staircases.

A

True.
Other culinary traditions put sauces on their chips, but only Newfoundlanders add the dressing (stuffing made with bread crumbs and always including summer savoury).

Q

True or False:
For a brief period in the 1980s,
Newfoundland and Labrador's tourism
slogan was "Come Feel Our Warmth."

Q

What is a *quintal*
and how is the word pronounced?

A

False.
That somewhat suggestive slogan
was used by Prince Edward Island.

A

A *quintal* (pronounced *kintle*) is a
measure of 112 pounds used for fish.

Three men weighing salt fish, Battle Harbour, Labrador, 1909.
The Rooms Provincial Archives Division, VA 103-6.3

Q

What is the most common family name
on the island of Newfoundland?

Q

How would a hunter use this implement?

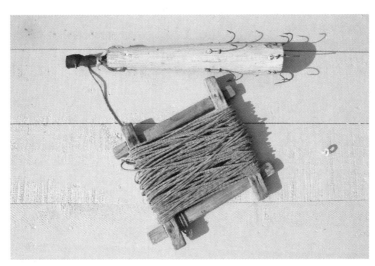

A

White, possibly because it occurs among
Newfoundlanders with both English and
Irish roots. Other common names tend to
occur among one group or the other:
Parsons is usually Protestant; Power, Catholic.

A

The implement is a bird jigger,
used to retrieve shot seabirds.

Q

True or False:
Elements of the Screech-in can be traced
to United States naval tradition.

A

True.
In the mid-1970s, Fred Walsh
created the "Screech Club" to entertain
tourists at a St. John's nightclub. Walsh had
been manager of the Officers' Club at the
Argentia naval base, where he witnessed the
"Crossing the Line" ceremony, a hazing ritual.
There are strong resemblances between the
two ceremonies.

Crossing the Line ceremony aboard HMAS *Melbourne. Wiki-media Commons*

CITY OF
LEGENDS

Q

True or False:
The "jelly-bean" colours of downtown
St. John's houses are not traditional.

Q

True or False:
In 1967, the Summer of Love,
St. John's City Council rejected
a proposal to rename Military Road
"Avenue of Peace."

A

True.
The colour scheme was proposed
in 1977 by the St. John's Heritage
Foundation in an effort to brighten the
"grim" look of downtown housing.
Houses were traditionally painted in
dark colours, with no contrasting trim,
probably because it was cheaper.

A

False.
(But they would have, because the idea
would have come from young people.)

Q

True or False:
Regatta Day in St. John's is the only movable,
weather-dependent civic holiday in North America.

Q

True or False:
Two years after the Summer of Love, a
section of Water Street was closed to traffic and
converted to a pedestrian mall for the summer.

A

True.

A

True.
During the summer of 1969, Water Street
was closed to traffic from Prescott Street
to McBride's Hill, and trees, flowers, grass,
and park benches were installed. At the
end of the summer, some business own-
ers complained that sales had decreased
and the experiment was deemed a failure.
Original photo Joe Chua. (Hippies
added by John Andrews.)

Q

True or False:
In a 2016 in-house survey, 93 per cent of
Royal Newfoundland Constabulary
officers agreed with the statement
"St. John's drivers are idiots."

Q

In 1951 an engineer's report on
a proposed major construction
project cautioned, "Do what you will
architecturally, brick is still brick and
suggests a factory." What was the project?

A

False.
There was no such survey. (But the
results would probably have been
similar if there had been a survey.)

A

Memorial University's new campus on
Elizabeth Avenue. Professor H.R. Theak-
ston's recommendation was to use Kelly's
Island sandstone for its natural beauty.
The recommendation was ignored.

Q

The largest section of the St. John's
Yellow Pages is Restaurants.
What's the second largest?

Q

Where is the other Cabot Tower?

A

Lawyers.
(It used to be Escort Services,
before the Internet.)

A

Bristol, England. It was built for the same
reason as the smaller St. John's tower, to mark
the 400th anniversary of Zuan Caboto's voyage
to Newfoundland. Bristol's tower was completed
in 1898, two years before Newfoundland's. Both
towers include machicolations, a feature of castles
that allows boiling oil to be poured on attackers.

Cabot Tower, Bristol. *Wikimedia
Commons/Adrian Pingstone/CC-SA-3.0*

Q

What was the original name of the Regatta
Day tune often called "Up the Pond"?

Q

What is the meaning of this
announcement sometimes heard on
morning radio in St. John's:
"The *Flanders* is solo on the Tickle."

A

"The Banks of Newfoundland"
(composed around 1820 by the chief
justice of Newfoundland, Francis Forbes)

A

The ferry *Flanders* is the
only ferry operating on the
Portugal Cove-Bell Island run.

Q

Which, if any, of these statements
is demonstrably true?

a. St. John's is the oldest city in North
America
b. St. John's is the oldest city in North
America, if you exclude Mexico
c. St. John's is the oldest city in North
America, if you exclude the Caribbean
d. St. John's is the oldest city in North
America, if you exclude Florida
e. St. John's is one of the oldest European
settlements in the western hemisphere

A

e. is the only one you can defend on really solid ground. It's tangly, of course, and depends on what you mean by "city" and whether the place is still occupied, but contenders for the title include:

Cholula, Mexico—circa 500 BCE
Mexico City—1325
Santo Domingo—1498
Saint Augustine, Florida—1565
Quebec City—1608
St. John's, Newfoundland—post-1630

But St. John's is, after all, the City of Legends. Of course, all of this counts for nothing if you "develop" your city with reckless disregard for everything that's old about it. Some cities have been more imaginative in this regard than others.

Q

True or False:
During World War II the Canadian government drafted a secret contingency plan to set fire to buildings and wharves in St. John's Harbour and open the valves on the Southside fuel tanks.

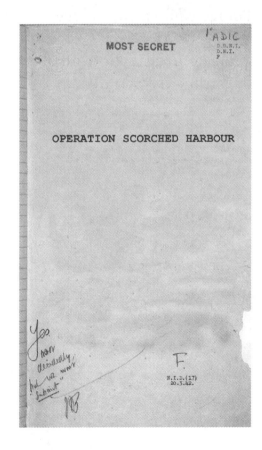

A

True.

The plan was to be used in case the Germans seized St. John's Harbour, which would have been a prime beachhead for an attack on North America. Burning would deprive the enemy of valuable buildings, equipment, and fuel. The risk to the largely wooden city was considered acceptable. (The report cover is a fake, courtesy Gerry Porter.)

What do these St. John's statues
have in common?

A

The statue of explorer Gaspar Corte-Real near Confederation Building and the statue of Our Lady of Fatima in the Basilica of St. John the Baptist were both gifts from the people of Portugal.

Q

True or False:
The largest Art Deco building constructed
in 20th-century Newfoundland was built for
the Total Abstinence and Benefit Society.

A

True.

After the Society sold the building, it became the home of CBC Radio, which at the time was regarded by some as ironic. CBC Radio moved uptown in 2007 after more than 50 years in the central location, much to the dismay of some old hands. The building was left vacant, awaiting redevelopment as a condo building.

CBC

GRAB BAG

Q

If you encounter a coyote in the wild, which response would be the wrong thing to do?

a. Wave your arms and shout
b. Blow a loud whistle
c. Run away as fast as you can
d. Throw rocks or sticks at it
e. Club it with a walking stick

Christopher Bruno

A

c. Don't run. Coyotes are like dogs: they instinctively chase anything that runs away (like a dog chasing a tennis ball). Running away would be pointless, as coyotes have been clocked at 60 kilometres per hour.

The Provincial Wildlife Division has a helpful online guide to living with coyotes. It advises walking away quietly if the coyote hasn't seen you, but otherwise reacting aggressively: "If the coyote attacks you, fight back"—a daunting prospect.

Q

What Newfoundland attraction was rated one of the Ten Best Adventure Destinations in the world by *National Geographic* in 2012?

A

The East Coast Trail.

Cobbler Path. *Mary Smyth and Fred Hollingshurst*

Q

The Long Range Mountains are part
of what mountain chain?

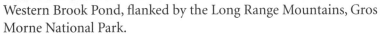
Western Brook Pond, flanked by the Long Range Mountains, Gros
Morne National Park.

A

The Appalachians.

John W. Doyle

Q

What's wrong with this sign?

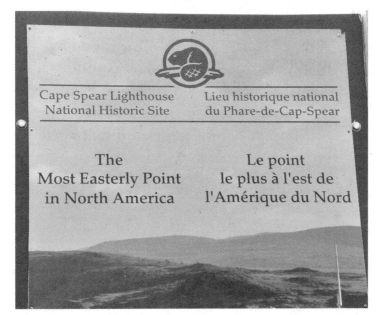

Cape Spear Lighthouse
National Historic Site

Lieu historique national
du Phare-de-Cap-Spear

The
Most Easterly Point
in North America

Le point
le plus à l'est de
l'Amérique du Nord

A

It's not true. Nordostrundingen, Greenland, is the most easterly point. Geographers consider Greenland to be one of North America's "surrounding islands." If you only consider continental North America, then Newfoundland is also excluded and the most easterly point is Cape Saint Charles, Labrador.

Q

True or False:
All of the estimated 150,000 moose
in Newfoundland today are
descended from just four ancestors.

Rocky Grimes

A

True (probably). Four moose were brought to the island from New Brunswick in 1904 and set free near Howley. There were originally seven, but three died while waiting for the boat to Port aux Basques. (This may sound familiar to anyone who has tried to take the Gulf ferry in high summer.) The moose were allowed to breed without being hunted for 30 years and did really, really well. (At least there was no legal hunt. There are reports that Newfoundlanders quickly developed a taste for the vegetarian ruminants.)

Why probably? An earlier attempt to introduce moose was made in 1878, when two animals were transported from Nova Scotia, but it is generally believed that the pair did not breed.

Q

How do you pronounce *Quirpon*,
a community and an island on the tip
of the Northern Peninsula?

a. Rhymes with *gherkin*
b. Rhymes with *harpoon*
c. Rhymes with *upon*

A

b. *Quirpon* rhymes with *harpoon*. The community may be named after Le Kerpont in Brittany, which it is said to resemble. The name has been used to test the local knowledge of would-be TV and radio announcers.

Q

What's wrong with this picture?

A

It's actually Trimmed *Navel* Beef, meaning beef from the cow's navel area rather than beef preserved for long naval voyages. The trimming is fortuitous as no one wants to find a cow's belly button in their Jiggs' dinner.

Of course another answer would be that it may not be a great idea to consume a food whose 100-gram standard serving size contains 142 per cent of the recommended daily intake of sodium.

Q

Why is a traditional Newfoundland boiled
dinner sometimes called *Jiggs' dinner*?

a. It's named after a comic strip character
b. It's often served at dances
c. It's standard fare aboard fishing trawlers
d. It's a corruption of the Irish word
   jaíochs meaning "pudgy"
e. It's named after a character in a
   Newfoundland folk tale

A

a. Corned beef and cabbage was the favourite meal of Jiggs, a character in the comic strip *Bringing Up Father* which was widely syndicated in North American newspapers in the early 20th century.

Q

What is the obscured word on this
Newfoundland stamp?

A

"Currency."
Both stamp and fish have
become collector's items.

Bigstock photo

Q

True or False:
Memorial University's tunnel system
(the "Munnel") is unique among
North American universities.

Q

Why do you never see cod sushi
on a menu?

A

False.
A number of other universities have similar systems, including University of Manitoba, Carleton, and McGill. A Lutheran college in Mequon, Wisconsin, has nearly 4 miles of tunnels.

A

Cod often carry a worm which is killed by cooking.

Q

Where does Newfoundland rank among
the largest islands in the world?

a. Top 10
b. Top 20

Q

What does the acronym *NONIA* stand for?

A

b. Newfoundland is 16th in area, smaller than Great Britain, larger than Cuba.

A

Newfoundland Outport Nursing and Industrial Association. In the early 20th century women living in outports made knitted goods that were sold to raise money to help pay for public health nurses. Today NONIA continues as a non-profit cottage industry with nearly 200 knitters throughout the province.

Q

What was a Newfoundland child psychologist talking about when she said this, in 1988: "My main concern is that it's very disruptive to children. Getting children to go to bed at a reasonable hour so that they're not irritable the next day is one of the main problems."

A

Double Daylight Saving Time, which the province introduced as an experiment in the summer of 1988. Newfoundland was the first, and still the only, place in North America to adopt the unusual time zone. The idea was rumoured to be the brainchild of the culture minister at the time, Bill Matthews, whose riding included a big soccer town.

Ten years later a member of the House of Assembly recalled the chaos: "We were up all night, all day; we could not get to sleep. You could not get a coffee in the morning at Tim Horton's because there was no coffee; there was no morning." The member was Beaton Tulk, who would later become the seventh premier of the province.

DDST was quietly shelved after one summer.

Q

What modern names have replaced these
old community names?

a. Scilly Cove
b. Damn the Bell Bay
c. Gayside
d. Squid Tickles
e. Bumble Bee Bight
f. Toad's Cove
g. Famish Gut

A

a. Winterton
b. St. Chad's
c. Baytona
d. Burnside
e. Pilley's Island
f. Tors Cove
g. Fair Haven

Q

What was formerly located at this site on the Trans-Canada Highway roughly halfway between Badger and Grand Falls-Windsor?

Trans-Canada Highway

A

Pearson's Peak, a monument erected
in 1966 to mark the completion of the
Trans-Canada Highway in Newfoundland.
The pillar eventually fell into disrepair
and was demolished for fear that rocks
would fall on courting couples who
were parking in the area.

Archives and Special Collections Division, J.R. Smallwood Collection,
Coll. 075, 5.04.99, 5.04.5600

Q

Which of these communities is closest to the geographic centre of Newfoundland?

a. Bishop's Falls
b. Gander
c. Grand Falls-Windsor
d. Lewisporte
e. Millertown

Q

True or False:
Filleting a fish is not as difficult
as it's made out to be.

Q

True or False: Newfoundland is the
only jurisdiction in the world with a
half-hour time zone.

A

c. Grand Falls-Windsor.

A

False.
It takes considerable skill to fillet a cod
without wasting half the fish, leaving in
bones, or slicing your hand.

A

False. Other places on half-hour time
zones include India, Afghanistan, and
North Korea. Nepal's time zone is offset by
45 minutes.

Q

True or False:
Most moose-vehicle collisions are fatal.

Q

Which of these was the largest
construction project undertaken in
Newfoundland in the 19th century?

a. H.M. Penitentiary, St. John's
b. The Colonial Building
c. Bowaters Paper Mill, Corner Brook
d. R.C. Cathedral of St. John the Baptist
e. Waterford Hospital

A

True, for the moose.
Drivers and passengers fare much
better, but there are several hundred
moose collisions in Newfoundland
every year, and some result in serious
injury or death.

A

d. R.C. Cathedral of St. John the Baptist
(now the Basilica).

Q

What Newfoundland folk song
is quoted in the lyrics of the
Shanneyganock hit "The Islander"?

Q

True or False:
If you are lost in the woods in
Newfoundland, it helps to remember
that lichens grow more profusely
on the north sides of trees.

A

"Jack Was Every Inch a Sailor"

"The Islander" by Bruce Moss:
In Montreal the Frenchmen say
that they own Labrador
Including Indian Harbour,
where me father fished before.

"Jack Was Every Inch a Sailor":
When Jack grew up to be a man
he went to Labrador,
And fished in Indian Harbour
where his father fished before.

A

True.
Lichens like moisture, and the north side
of a tree is less likely to dry out since it's
not exposed to the sun. But a compass or
GPS would be even more helpful.